IMAGES OF ENGLAND

KIDDERMINSTER
THE SECOND SELECTION

IMAGES OF ENGLAND

KIDDERMINSTER
THE SECOND SELECTION

ROBERT BARBER

The
History
Press

The Raven, No. 103 Bromsgrove Street. The pub opened around 1840 and closed 7 September 1969, at the time of the Bromsgrove Street house clearance scheme.

Frontispiece: A report in the *Kidderminster Shuttle* of 9 January 1937 related a great discussion at the last meeting of the town council regarding the suggested moving of Richard Baxter's statue to improve the traffic flow through the Bull Ring. It was finally moved in 1967 to the ring road outside St Mary's church. Sir George Eddy who had been a lifelong campaigner for the removal of the statue can be seen in the dark coat to the right of the statue – everything comes to he who waits.

First published 2002

Reprinted in 2014 by
The History Press
The Mill, Brimscombe Port,
Stroud, Gloucestershire, GL5 2QG
www.thehistorypress.co.uk

British Library Cataloguing in Publication Data.
A catalogue record for this book is available from the British Library.

ISBN 978 0 7524 2619 8

Typesetting and origination by
Tempus Publishing Limited.
Printed and bound in Great Britain by
Marston Book Services Limited, Oxfordshire

Contents

Elephants were marched from the railway station, down Comberton Hill and along Green Street when the circus came to town in August 1962.

Foreword

It gives me pleasure to write the foreword for Robert Barber's second book illustrating some of the changes and events that have taken place in Kidderminster.

I joined the engineers and surveyors department of Kidderminster Borough Council in 1950. A tremendous amount of work was undertaken from that time until being incorporated into the Wyre Forest District in 1974.

The post-war priority was the provision of much needed council housing, with over 3,000 dwellings being constructed on the new estates. There were also industrial developments, a new cattle market, and improvements to municipal buildings, highways, sewers and water works. The emphasis then turned to the town centre when the ring road was constructed to divert traffic away from the narrow town centre streets, followed by the development of the Swan Centre and Rowland Hill shopping precincts.

A considerable amount of research has been done to accompany the illustrations and use has been made of Borough photographs taken at the time of construction.

It is amazing how quickly the memory of these upheavals in the town can be forgotten, particularly when many of the central factories and the more recently constructed multi-storey car parks and cattle market have been demolished to make way for other developments.

Robert Barber's latest book will be an interesting and useful record of the reshaping of the town, past events, and personalities.

Jeff Higgott
Former Associate Borough Engineer and Surveyor

Introduction

Since the first Kidderminster book in the *Images of England* series, the changes to our town of Kidderminster have been quite unprecedented. My humble advice to anyone considering producing a book on the area is to get a camera and take some local shots, then sit back for a couple of years and you will probably find you have a good basis for a book! That is how it seems when you walk along Corporation Street, Market Street, or Green Street. I have used photographs of these areas, some of which were only taken twelve months ago, but within a very short time the memories of them will start to fade, and a short while longer there will be people who don't remember them at all.

Away from the town centre at Foley Park, the Sugar Factory has recently closed after seventy-seven years of beet campaigns with vehicles descending on Kidderminster from all directions laden with beet.

S.D.F. Saturday 2nd Team, Kidderminster League 1961/62. From left to right, back row: J. Wagstaff, Pountney, G. Bytheway, M. Preece, A. Yates, T. Faulks, G. Edwards, W. Sherriff (manager). Front row: P. Royle, J. Stancer, M. Thompson, G. Parmenter, G. Owen.

S.D.F. is one of the large employers who have disappeared from Kidderminster. They commenced operations on the Stourport Road at the end of the Second World War, at the same time that the Birchen Coppice Estate was being built, which is where a lot of the workforce would have lived. They had excellent social facilities for the employees, and a large sports field, that has now sadly been swallowed up by industrial units.

In addition to factories closing or moving, we have lost two multi-storey car parks which really is a pity because they have provided great vantage points for taking photographs of the town over the years, as well as providing good parking facilities, though perhaps I'm being selfish.

I have lived in and around Kidderminster all my life but until I saw some of the photographs, which I have been very fortunate to use, I had quite forgotten how a lot of the town used to look.

There is one exception to all these changes; the last chapter looks at one small part of Kidderminster that has survived for nearly 700 years, which in a town like ours is quite an achievement.

I hope that whomever looks at this little book, whether they buy it or borrow it, will enjoy rediscovering the past illustrated in these pages as much as I did.

Robert Barber
April 2002

One

The Sugar Factory

Campaign time, with the lorries loaded with beet queuing to offload, *c.* 1960.

Clement Dalley and his family at The Cedars, Kidderminster, 1898. From left to right, back row: Winnie Dalley (later Vale), Clement Dalley, Mrs Jane Dalley. Front row: Mrs Betty Pound (servant/housekeeper and lifelong friend), Clement W. Dalley (killed in the First World War), Frances Dalley (later Vaudin), Reg Dalley (joint founder of Doolittle & Dalley), Edith Dalley (later Gethin). As early as 1894 Clement Dalley was investigating the possibility of setting up a beet sugar works in Kidderminster. He owned a successful corn and seed business in the town so everything he could do to assist the farmers was to all their advantages. In 1898 successful sugar beet growing trials had been carried out at eleven farms in the area; of these eight samples were of a higher purity than the 80% required in the United States and the overall average was 82.38%.

Dalley's Corner, New Road, with the Bay Horse Inn to the left of the picture. Dalley's was one of the first buildings in Kidderminster to be constructed with reinforced concrete. A German scientist named Andreas Marggraf had discovered how to extract sugar from the sugar beet root in 1748, with the first beet sugar factory being built in 1799 at Breslau, which is the German name for Wroclaw, in Poland. During the Napoleonic wars the British Navy's blockading of the French ports resulted in the country being starved of their sugar imports. Sugar at this time was produced from sugar cane grown in the European colonies. As a result of the British blockade Napoleon decreed that the French farmers should grow sugar beet; sugar imports were thereby banned and state assistance was given, resulting in France producing over 3,000 tons of sugar from 300 plus factories by 1813. It was to be almost 100 years before this country started producing its own sugar, and then in a modest way, with the first factory being built by the Dutch at Cantley, Norfolk, in 1912. During the 1920s seventeen factories were built in this country with the sugar factory at Kidderminster being built in 1925. The majority of the factories were limited to processing 500 tons of beet per day, which was in line with French practice. However, within a very short time they were upgraded to 1,000 tons capability including Kidderminster.

Directors of the West Midland Sugar Company, 6 June 1925. From left to right: G.R. Woodward, J.B. Talbot-Crosbie, Hon. A.A. Vanneck, Georgina Brinton, H. Wigse, C.C. Brinton, Rt Hon. Lord Weir.

On 17 April 1925 the site at Foley Park was chosen for a number of reasons. Firstly it was a large, relatively flat site, with a good foundation of sandstone close to the surface, (this was needed to support the heavy machinery required for sugar production) and was close to the GWR line linking the Oxford, Worcester, and Wolverhampton lines to the Severn Valley line. The site was also close to the Stourport Road, which was made into a dual carriageway after the factory was built to accommodate the transport bringing the beet to the factory. Secondly, the site was close to a water supply. The river Stour is nearby and a well was sunk on the site (a plant the size of Kidderminster needs up to 3 million gallons of water per day). Thirdly, the commitment of the local farmers and the N.F.U. to guarantee beet supplies was also needed and obtained. At long last the government of the day had realized the need for the country to be able to produce its own sugar, in the main due to the fact that demand had outstripped supply with the result that sugar had become a very expensive commodity. Farmers were also struggling and land was falling into neglect. In 1922 they remitted excise duty on sugar, and in 1924 the government announced further proposals, which were embodied into the 1925 Sugar-Industry (subsidy) Act. The government also provided loan guarantees under the Trade Facilities Acts 1921-26. As a result of all these measures a further seventeen factories were built during the 1920s.

The railway sidings being laid down, 1 May 1925. A GWR saddle tank engine, which was one of many owned by the company, can be seen in the background.

Rolling stock from the days of nationalization. In 1925 85% of sugar beet was transported by rail, 12% by road and 3% by water. However by 1930 53% was transported by rail, 44% by road and 3% by water. The Kidderminster factory covers the south-west area of the country but in the early days the beet was supplied to the factory from mostly local growers. As transport and roads have improved over the years however sugar beet has been brought to Kidderminster from as far away as Devon, and Cornwall. British Sugar gives the farmers sugar beet quotas so they know whatever they grow up to that quota will be purchased; this gives them a certain amount of stability. With the closure of the Kidderminster factory the local growers were obviously going to incur extra transport costs so a subsidy was granted to cover these extra costs, but only lasted for three years.

The steel structure nearing completion, 6 June 1925. The main contractors employed were Thomas Vale and sons.

Power House, the original turbine and alternator installation, 29 August 1925. Electric power was used from the start and initially only one chimney was required; the factory was therefore self-sufficient in water and electricity. This was very important during the campaign (especially the electricity) when the factory ran for sixteen weeks, twenty-four hours a day. In these circumstances power cuts would have been a distict possibility if they had been dependent on the national grid, and this would have been inconvenient to say the least. The combined heat and power design of a sugar factory makes it 80% efficient. A power station runs at about 40% efficiency. The generators in use at the time the factory ceased operations could produce 7MW.

William J. Logan (sugar boiler, left) and Charlie Potts (pan helper). One of the first problems that would have confronted the West Midland Sugar Co. would have been locating and employing sugar boilers. There had been no sugar factories in Kidderminster before 1925 and sugar boiling was not a skill that could be learnt in a few weeks. There were sugar boilers in Scotland however and that is where the Kidderminster Co. went looking, obviously with the co-operation of the Anglo Scottish Beet Sugar Corporation to whom they were amalgamated. Five of the original sugar boilers were: F. Boyle, J. Frizell, S. Macaulay, W. Ireland, and W.J. Logan. Mr Logan had been employed by John Walker and Co. of Greenock, near Port Glasgow, Scotland, and a letter of introduction dated 12 January 1922 stated he had been employed by the firm as a sugar boiler since July 1917, completing a four-year apprenticeship. They had pleasure in recommending him for the situation for which he was applying. In addition to the good rates of pay, houses were built on the factory site and offered to the sugar boilers for as long as they were employed by the company. They were obviously determined to get these important employees, who were of course essential to the sugar plant. Correspondence to Mr Logan dated 29 October 1927 was addressed to the Anglo Scottish Beet Sugar Corporation Ltd, Colwick, Nottingham, but from 21 June 1928 they were from West Midland Sugar Company Ltd.

Laying the tracks, 21 April 1925. When the factory was built it was able to process 500 tons of beet per day. This had risen to 1,200 tons by 1930-31, 2,900 tons by 1975, and nearly 5,000 tons by 1992. This was ten times the initial processing capability, achieved mainly by more efficient working practices and new equipment.

An aerial view of the factory, c. 1926. At the top of the picture is the site of the Birchen Coppice Estate, which was not built until some twenty years later. A large majority of the workforce would have probably lived here.

Sugar boilers houses. Mr Logan's house was on the left of the second block.

Probably one of the first group photographs of the workforce, pictured outside No. 1 sugar warehouse, end of main building with the boiler house on the right. The sugar warehouse burned down in later years, probably in the early 1970s, requiring it to be rebuilt.

Kidderminster and District Bowling League Champions, 1933. From left to right, back row: W. Ireland, J. Anderson, R. Lawson, S. Skelding, S. Macaulay, F. Vale, J. Mann, S. Brooks, T. Trinder, O. Savery. Front row: G. Bright, J. Slater, W. Logan, A. Jacobs, E. Kirkby, A. Smith, F. Bidmead. Mr Logan was a keen bowler and was a founder member of the area's midweek bowls league in 1933.

A more informal group shot, from left to right: Jack Wagstaff, Stan Goode, Bob Roberts (kneeling). Jack commenced work for the Sugar Factory in 1945 as an engine shunter, later becoming a charge hand in the pulp store. He completed twenty-eight years with the company, retiring in 1973.

The beet is brought into the factory and the loads are weighed; a sample of beet is taken to ascertain the sugar content (17% on average) and the amount of soil, stones, weed etc. This determined how much the farmer received for the load.

The beet is unloaded into the silos where it is washed and propelled along its way by jets of water in channels known as flumes. The majority of the lorries used today are of the tip up variety so it is doubtful if you would see beets being unloaded by hand.

The beet wheel was used to separate the beet from the transport water when flumes fed the factory. A belt later replaced this.

The Kidderminster factory supplied domestic as well as industrial sugars up until the 1990s. This was the domestic sugar-packaging department.

This was a committee made up of shop floor workers and management to discuss any internal problems that would crop up from time to time, ranging from technical, to health and safety issues. From left to right, back row: H. Lamb (yard foreman), H. Millward (evaps man), J. Millman (engineer), J. Hatton (tin smith), A. Lamb (welder). Front row: W. Logan (sugar boiler), E. Kirkby (general manager), A. Richardson (factory manager), R. Devitt (assistant manager).

The original weighbridge.

Number 4 sugar warehouse showing bulk pile and portable conveyors. There would have been around 15,000 tons of sugar in the stack. In the last years of the Kidderminster factory the way of storing the sugar was changed after a near fatal accident.

The factory during one of the campaigns in the 1960s, taken from the sports field. Offices are on the left, animal feed and dryer-house in the centre and main building and boiler stack to right.

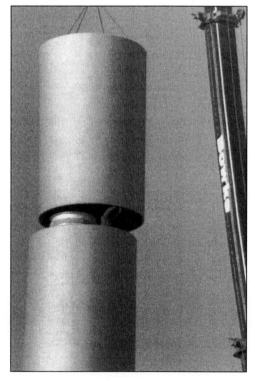

Left: The lime kiln. *Right*: The chimney erected in the 1990s. The steam seen pouring forth on cold winter days was from the cattle feed drying process

After the chimney was completed it became a well-known landmark, especially during the campaign when its large white cloud of steam billowed forth.

The silos, which are used for storing refined sugar, were constructed in 1972. They could hold 12,000 tons each.

The Sugar Factory was a landmark from all directions. This view is from Blackwell Street car park in February 2001 when the factory was approaching the end of its penultimate campaign.

For most of the year all seemed quiet as you passed by the factory, then every October the whole place would come alive when lorries and tractors laden with beets would descend on the Stourport Road from all directions of south-west England and Wales. The clouds of steam pouring from the tall chimney, and the strong familiar smell would fill your nostrils, and people would forecast the weather if they could smell the beet.

The majority of people alive today who have been born and bred in Kidderminster have always known a sugar factory on the Stourport Road, it's another of those little parts of Kidderminster that have gone forever.

Two

Council Services, Water and Housing

Kidderminster's first council house. There is a foundation stone laid by Alderman Griffin celebrating the occasion.

Originally the water supply for the town came from a well and a borehole on the Stourport Road in the Foley Park area. They had been sunk to a depth of 600ft, (183 metres), the scheme being installed between 1870-74. Prior to this time people living in the town obtained their water from wells, Broadwaters pool, and the Cape Inn in New Road, which had a pump. There were also water sellers; these people would collect water from streams (Blakebrook being a popular source), and take the water round to the dwellings on their carts. The majority of these water supplies were contaminated, and this obviously resulted in a lot of sickness and disease causing the death rate to rise to 35 in 1,000 in 1868.

The Pumping Station, Green Street, erected in 1905.

Wells were sunk in Green Street in the late nineteenth century and were used to supply the town in 1879, when the pumps at Foley Park had to be stopped for repairs. The use of these wells was found to be more cost effective and so the arrangement was continued. In 1898 a third well was sunk in Green Street, and by March 1905 the last stage of the scheme perfecting the towns water supply was under way with the contractors Thomas Vale & Co. The borough surveyor, the late Mr Arthur Comber C. E. (who incidentally was born at The Greyhound, Franche), had been the brains behind the scheme, but his premature death in 1900, at the age of forty-nine, caused the work to be greatly delayed. Some of the work had already been carried out however; a new well was sunk with a borehole of 30cm diameter, to a depth of nearly 125m. It was believed the town would obtain a splendid supply of pure water. Just prior to these events the company of Mr George Law had laid a rising main from the Green Street Works to the reservoir near Foley Park. This enabled all the water raised from the wells to be pumped into the reservoir instead of directly into the towns mains, as was the case until that time.

Messrs Vale & Company were contracted to erect the engine house in Green Street on the site of the new well. The laying of the foundations was particularly difficult because of the running sand that had to be removed to a depth of 5m before rock was reached. A boiler house with stack was also to be erected on the other side of Green Street, close to the pump house. The steam pipes were laid under the road and new mains had to be laid in certain parts of the town. The engine had already been ordered from Barclay Son & Company of Kilmarnock by this time, and when it was finally installed it proved to be a very handsome one with a large flywheel that could be observed through the pump house window slowly turning. When the Green Street Pumping Station was completed it was intended to be used as a reserve in emergencies only, but most of the borough was supplied from this well after 1908. In the 1930s an electric pump was installed to take over the increasing workload with the steam pump being kept in reserve as a back up.

This is the large wheel of the pump that could be observed through the window of the pump house.

The steam pump was maintained in an immaculate condition, the pump house employees obviously taking a great pride in their work.

In the late 1950s the decision was taken to install a second electric pump to cope with the extra demand for water from the carpet factories and the people who were now living in the area due to the number of houses that had been built since the Second World War. At peak demand times the water level in the well would drop causing the original electric pump to work inefficiently and this in turn caused the water pressure to drop. Notice was given under the direction of J.G. Stewart, Borough Engineer and Surveyor for contractors to tender for the work which was to include breaking through the bottom of the existing well and sinking a 52.5 cm diameter bore hole 21m deep. It was to be steel lined for the first 15m and inter-connect with the existing borehole. A test pumping was to be carried out on completion. It was to be a fixed cost tender with no price variation being allowed for labour or materials, so the firms submitting the tenders needed to get their sums right. Tenders were to be submitted no later than first post on Monday 23 February 1959 and the work was to be completed within four weeks. It had been estimated that the cost of purchasing water from another authority while the town supply was out of action, was £80 per day, for which the successful contractor would be liable for every day the contracted work went over the four-week period. The site was to be made available to the successful contractor for 24 hours per day including weekends, and the completion of the work was not to be certified until the 48-hour pumping test of 65,000 gallons per hour, with the water level not falling lower than 18m below the floor level, had been completed.

As a result of the proposals the steam pump had to be dismantled and removed to make way for the new pump. According to Jeff Higgott, the assistant borough surveyor at the time, the people who had been responsible for the care and maintenance of the steam pump were extremely upset that their pride and joy was going to be cut up and sent to the scrap yard. Somehow an electric pump just hasn't got the same appeal.

It was decided to cut the wheel up into smaller sections to make it easier to remove from the building, and be transported by road.

I've started so I'll finish.

The jumbled remains
of the steam pump.

After some fifty-five years the pump is gradually removed from the building.

...piece by piece. This was the hub of the flywheel. It appears that the weather was in sympathy with the feelings of the pump house employees.

The well was deepened prior to the new pump being installed.

The water level in the well was continually dropping because of the extra demand for water, especially from the carpet factories. This is the second borehole being drilled.

After the second borehole had been drilled it was decided that the best way to connect the two boreholes was to insert an explosive charge into the borehole. The first charge was put in place but was unsuccessful. A second charge was inserted and this time was a success, the explosion causing the water to cascade over the top. There were sighs of relief all round.

The associate borough engineer and surveyor, H.J. Higgott, FICE (Fellow of the Institute of Chartered Engineers), poses with the newly-installed pump.

The new pump all installed and ready to extract the 65,000 gallons per hour.

Council Housing

The first council houses in Kidderminster were built between 1920-22 at Gheluvelt Avenue, Hurcott Road and Worcester Road. The average cost of these houses was £1,048 per house. Of these houses forty-four were four-bedroomed and included a parlour, and forty were three-bedroomed without a parlour. The total cost of the scheme was £88,000 and the rents amounted to 9s 9d and 6s 6d per week respectively. These first council houses were very costly because sixteen years later some four-bedroomed houses were built on Foley Park Estate at a cost of £374 each and a rent of 6s. Total cost of the Foley Park Estate, which was a total of 217 houses, was £72,000. The fact that sixteen years later the council could build an extra 133 houses for £16,000 less, seems quite amazing. The first council house in the borough was at No. 69 Hurcott Road. In 1936 the council built the 1,000th house, and by 1973 some 4,653 council houses had been built (3,400 since the Second World War). Birchen Coppice was the first council estate to be built after the Second World War, comprised of 661 houses.

Jubilee Drive, Foley Park Estate. The house on the right was the 1,000th council house to be built in Kidderminster. The borough council certainly rose to the challenge of the need for council housing after the war, with the 1950s seeing more council estates being built at Franche, Comberton, Habberley, and Broad Street. Habberley Estate was the largest project, comprised of 735 houses built between 1956-59. Then came Hurcott Road again with 189 houses in 1963-67, the Rifle Range, and Hoo Brook. In 1967 Comberton Estate was started and when completed was the largest council estate in Kidderminster.

Broadwaters Estate viewed from Barnsley's Hill. In the years between 1933-34, three-bedroomed non-parlour houses were built, at an average cost of £326 per house. The approximate total cost of houses, land, roads, and sewers was £75,000. Rents in 1936 were 5s 6d per week.

Foley Park Estate was built 1934-36 at a total cost of £72,000. The estate consisted of twenty-four one-bedroomed bungalows, 147 three-bedroomed houses, forty-six four-bedroomed (all non parlour) at costs of £250, £332 and £374 respectively. These were unusual blocks of four three-bedroom houses. Rents in 1936 varied from 2s 11d to 6s per week.

This is part of Sutton Farm Estate and was built between 1926-33 and consisted of 412 houses in the area of Sutton Farm, Greatfield Road, and Sutton Common. Total cost was £162,000. House types were 172 three-bedroom (with parlour) costing £437; 182 three-bedroom (non parlour) costing £370 and fifty-eight two-bedroomed (non parlour) costing £336. Rent in 1936 was from 5s to 7s 5d per week.

Alderman R.S. Brinton, vice-chairman of Town Planning and Housing Committee 1917-1919 and chairman of Parks and Buildings Committee 1922-1930.

Aggborough Estate (Cobham Road) fronting Worcester Road. In 1932 fifty-eight three-bedroomed non-parlour houses were built costing £384 each. Total cost was £22,300. Rent in 1936 was 5s 6d per week.

Alderman T. Griffin, chairman of Health Committee 1924-36, chairman of Parks and Buildings Committee 1919-21 and co-founder and first chairman of the Empire Carpet Co.

Some people with secure occupations would choose the option to buy, but they were in the minority in the 1930s. This housing advertisement is from 24 June 1937.

Three

T. & A. Naylor

Fly Mill Reeling, 1960.

Messrs T. & A. Naylor started life in a modest way. Mr Richard Watson started a worsted-spinning mill at Drayton, Chaddesley Corbett, and in 1853 Joseph Naylor moved from Halifax and formed the partnership Watson and Naylor. Mr Naylor had already been engaged in textile spinning and the partnership proved to be successful, with the yarn produced being sold mainly to Kidderminster carpet manufacturers. Kidderminster was rapidly growing in importance as the carpet centre of the country and there was an abolition of import duties providing just the lift-off the new company needed.

Drayton Mill, 15 January 2002. The company soon outgrew the small premises at Drayton, and as a result of this, a large plot of ground was purchased at Green Street, where the Pike Mills were built, and modern worsted machinery was installed.

In around 1870 Joseph brought his two sons, Thomas and Arthur, into the business as partners. Not long afterwards, Richard Watson, who was the main shareholder, brought in his two sons, probably in a tit for tat move. This caused a a fair amount of friction and in 1883 the partnership between Watson and Naylor was dissolved, leaving the Naylors with the carpet and woollen spinning plant housed in Watson's premises.

A few years after Pike Mills had first been built they extended into Dixon Street and installed woollen spinning machinery to supply yarn for the increasing number of Royal and Chenille Axminster power looms. They also supplied 'Ingrain' carpet plant for the manufacture of 'Kidderminster Carpet'.

Joseph Naylor, Mayor of Kidderminster and founder of the firm.

A brief explanation of 'Kidderminster Carpet': in 1788 a factory was started in Kilmarnock for the manufacture of the common two-ply cloth, and other Scottish factories soon followed. In less than forty years, as people became more affluent, would-be customers were demanding a better quality carpeting to suit their better lifestyles. Kilmarnock responded in 1824 and succeeded in producing three-ply carpet instead of the old two-ply. This meant a thicker carpet was produced which also made possible the use of more colours thus enabling more varied patterns. The process was taken up throughout Scotland and Scotch carpeting became famous. The new method was also adopted in England where the goods were better known as 'Kidderminster Carpet'. In the early days the looms were narrow ones and the strips of fabric produced were sewn together into carpets. In America the name 'Ingrain' was adopted for the fabric.

Destruction by fire of the first Pike Mills, 1 July 1886. Watson and Naylor built the first Pike Mills in 1857; it was five storeys high and the walls were 70cm thick. A carding shed was added in 1866 and it appears that this is the area where the fire started. The fire was discovered at about 11.15 p.m. and by midnight it was apparent that the mill could not be saved. The Stourbridge and Worcester brigades assisted the Kidderminster Volunteer Brigade. The mill was left as a burnt-out shell, but the site was quickly cleared and a new mill built and in operation by September 1887.

Joseph Naylor, who had been mayor of Kidderminster, retired from active participation in 1883. Thomas Fox Naylor, JP, and Arthur Naylor took over the woollen spinning and manufacture of Kidderminster carpets, and after a short time added the production of Chenille carpets and rugs.

Joseph Naylor passed away in 1909 and a year later T. & A. Naylor was changed into a private limited company with all the shares being held by the family, with T.F. Naylor becoming the first chairman.

The company made blankets and other woollen fabrics for the War Office during the First World War which necessitated more extensions and additions.

The following eight photographs show the Pike Mills' First World War blanket manufacture.

Carding

Mule Spinning

Weaving the blankets, Chenille Weft loom?

Scouring

Drying

Raising. T. Naylor is on the right.

Packing

Despatch

At the end of the First World War the buildings in Pike Mills were no longer adequate and this led to the building of the premises at the Worcester Road end of Green Street. This is 1935 during the process of raising the roof of the 'Finished Goods' warehouse.

Jacks were inserted all around the building and the brickwork was gradually removed. The roof was then raised to the required level and new brickwork was inserted.

Staff outing to Llandridnod Wells, September 1925.

November 1960 saw the completion of a bridge across Green Street to serve as access to the warehouse extension. The picture on the right shows a view looking into the new bridge.

Foley Mill was erected at Foley Park in 1933.

Foley Mill in 1961 and the installing of the first spool gripper loom.

The last loom in Kidderminster used for the manufacture of 'Kidder Carpet' (Ingrain).

Kidderminster and District Cricket League Division B Champions, 1970. From left to right, back row: W. Cooper, R. Potter, M. Blackford, F. Radcliffe, K. Bayliss, L. Bishop. Front row: E. Mottram, M. Delo, G. Fawke, D. Hartwell (captain), K. Baker, D. Colwell, R. Pugh.

Naylor's Cricket Team, winners of the Carpet Weavers cup, 1960. From left to right, back row: W. Crowe, A. Morris, J. Pugh, D. Naylor, J. Rambo, J. Fisher, A. Commons, B. Etwell, K. Hartland. Front row: P. Hodges, S. Cole, J. Pearsall, J. Black, M. Dalo, R. Pugh, C. Bradley.

Naylor's winners of Division 4, 1960. They played twenty-four matches and won all of them. From left to right, back row: D. Parkes (trainer), P. Ince, J. Pearsall, M. Evans, R. Chance, -?-, G. Clee. Front row: F. Lawton, R. Potter, J. Black (who scored sixty-six goals), J. Pugh, E. Motteram, R. Pugh.

Division 4 netball champions, 1960. From left to right, back row: P. Oliver, J. Lewis, S. Waldron, P. Conolly. Front row: M. Danby, B. Fisher, M. Howles.

Naylor's appears to have been a happy firm with many long-serving employees. Jack Pugh (extreme left), Doris Jarvis and Walter Crowe (third from right) receive their forty years service awards.

The company continued to thrive for a number of years, this was a new Tufter they had installed at Lisle Avenue in 1966. However, by the time the 1970s arrived they had begun to struggle, making a loss one year and then a small profit the next. T. & A. Naylor went out of business in 1976 and Lionel Rowe who carried on producing carpets purchased the premises. Lionel Rowe moved to Wilden in 2000-01 with the old Naylor factory being demolished in 2001 as part of the redevelopment of the Green Street area of Kidderminster.

Carnival Dance, 1960.

The Gripper Loom with Mr C. Griffiths.

The demolition of Pike Mills, February 1968. The mill was demolished in 1968 as part of the town centre redevelopment; it had belonged to the Kidderminster Corporation since 1935.

Newspaper cuttings from the *Shuttle*, 1976.

Naylor's former factory in February 2001.

The former site, 15 January 2002.

From extension in 1953 (above) to destruction in 2001.

Four

The Castle Motor Company

The Castle Motor Company, started in 1907, soon became one of the most important garages in the area. They made a splendid effort at producing their own motor vehicle at the end of the First World War, but ultimately it was instrumental in their downfall. *Main picture:* the New Road premises. *Insets, clockwise from top left:* Laughton and Stanley Goodwin, the Vicar Street premises and the Castle Three.

Kidderminster (*continued*).

E. VII : *by Mill St. and Franche Rd.* :—
Quatt 9, **Bridgnorth** 14 (*v. gd. rd. hilly, 1/12 asc. at 2 m.*).

Lion, *High St.*, B 2/6 L 2/6 D 2/6 R 5/- Chfr 7/6 Shed ins M 1/-
N 1/6 Lion ⊤ 76.

Black Horse, *Mill St.*, B 2/6 L 2/6 D 3/6 R 3/6 Chfr 6/- Shed
ins *Gratis* RAC ⊤ Black Horse 186.

KIDDERMINSTER

SCALE

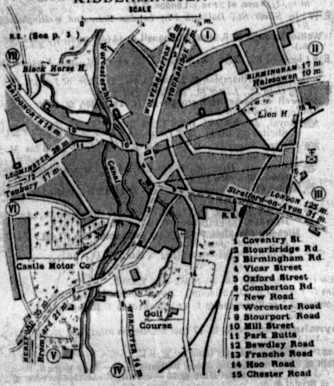

1 Coventry St.
2 Stourbridge Rd.
3 Birmingham Rd.
4 Vicar Street
5 Oxford Street
6 Comberton Rd.
7 New Road
8 Worcester Road
9 Stourport Road
10 Mill Street
11 Park Butts
12 Bewdley Road
13 Franche Road
14 Hoo Road
15 Chester Road

Michelin Stockists, **Castle Motor Co., Ltd.**, *New Rd.* and
19, Vicar St., Agts. for BELSIZE, FORD, ALLDAYS, SINGER
10 H.P., LU Sun., RAC ⊤ Castle Motor 113.

Kidwelly (Carmarthen), M. 16, (*M. 17, s. 4*), Pop. 3,035. E.C., *Wed.*
See :—Harbour ; Castle (XIth c., Rns.) ; St. Mary's Ch. (Goth.).
Carmarthen 10 = Llanelly 9, Swansea 20.

Kilbirnie (Ayr), M. 11, Pop. 4,571. E.C., *Wed.*
See :—W. Kilbirnie Place (Rns. XIVth c.) ; Church 1.
2 ⤙ Lochwinnoch 4, **Paisley** 14 — Beith 4 — Lochwinnoch 4, Kilmacolm 13 –
= Dalry 4, Kilwinning 9, Ardrossan 14 = Largs 9.
W. Clark, *Holmhead*, LU Sun., Night, ⊤ Clark.

Killin (Perth), M. 9, Pop. 537 (Alt. 360 ft.).
See :—N. Finlarig Cas. (Rns.) 1 ; Loch Tay.
Kenmore 17, Aberfeldy 23 = Ardeonaig 7, Kenmore 16, Aberfeldy
22 = Lix 3 ⤙ Lochearnhead 8, Callander 22 — Crianlarich 14,
Arrochar 33.
Killin, B 2/6 L 2/6 D 4/6 R 5/- Chfr 7/6 Gar LU ins N 1/-
SAC ⊤ Hotel.
H. J. Knight, Killin Hotel, Loch Tay.

The spare parts department with every one looking very serious except for the cheerful young man dressed like a bellhop – perhaps no one told him not to smile. The company prided themselves on having a large and comprehensive stock of spare parts.

In the years before the First World War, the company made good progress, they became one of the largest garages in the area, proficient in many aspects of the motor trade. They employed a large workforce, giving some of the local people an alternative to working in the carpet industry, which could be prone to short time working. They were in fact one of the pioneers of the motor industry.

The automatic machine shop.

Opposite: A page from the 1914 *Michelin Guide*. The Castle Motor Co. was the only garage included for Kidderminster.

All types of vehicles were accommodated from steam traction engines, from buses (above) to general road vehicles (below).

In the early days of the motor trade, some companies would design and fit vehicle bodies to pre-manufactured running chassis according to customers own requirements and specifications. The Castle Motor Company specialised in this area of the trade and was well renowned and respected in the district. When they went into manufacturing the Castle Three, just after the end of First World War, they were already well prepared for vehicle manufacture, but unfortunately not volume production.

A running chassis just delivered to the company. The delivery driver was exposed to the elements and everything that the wheels of other motor vehicles could throw at him.

The company built motor bodies to order and turned out some quite handsome examples, particularly on Essex and Hudson chassis. The body seen here is possibly a prototype for the Castle Three.

The bodies were sent to the assembly department to be fitted to the chassis.

Another part of the vehicle assembly building. The young man in the driving seat obviously fancies himself as a New York gangster.

The former premises in May 2001. The garage sign (inset) is still visible after more than seventy years.

The company had retail outlets in Vicar Street (*left*), Broad Street, Birmingham (*right*)...

... and this is the former site of the Worcester premises which for many years belonged to P.W. Wilde.

Commercial vehicle bodies were also designed and constructed.

With the advent of the First World War the company were seconded to manufacture munitions as part of the war effort. They were mainly engaged in the production of H.E. shells, depth charges, pistols, gun carriage hubs and components for the ABC Dragonfly engines.

This was one of the machine shops at the time of the First World War (shells to front left of picture). Notice the unguarded belts from the overhead driving gear; these would never pass today's stringent health and safety rules.

Shell cases produced by the company awaiting transportation to be filled with explosive.

During the first year of the war, shell contractors had obtained their steel from the makers, who had usually supplied them without any intervention from the government of the day. The specifications that determined the composition of shell steel, however, were rigid, and only two or three firms whose combined production amounted to about 5,000 tons per week could produce the steel of the quality required.

In a little over four years of war more than 196,000,000 rounds of gun ammunition were filled and completed in the factories of the British Isles, and another 21,000,000 in Canada and the United States of America, solely for the British Forces.

A small part of the workforce looking proud of their achievements.

To aid the war effort, women were employed in large numbers to do the work of the men who were away fighting. They proved to be just as efficient, no great surprise really.

By 1918, taking an average from all munitions factories, only 4% of the workforce was made up of skilled men; 82% of the workforce was made up of women and boys, and 14% unskilled men.

THE ENGINE, 4 Cylinder, Water-cooled

LIGHT TUBULAR CONNECTING ROD.

SOLID ONE-PIECE CAM SHAFT.

HEAVY CRANKSHAFT, MACHINED ALL OVER.

After the First World War Stanley Goodwin designed the Castle Three, which unfortunately was partly to blame for the eventual closure of the company. Above is illustrated one of the engine options and below the gearbox that was based on a Ford design. These are reproduced from the company brochure used to advertise the car.

GEAR BOX EPICYCLIC (Patent applied for)

TWO SPEEDS, FORWARD AND ONE REVERSE

NOTE—(1). The Unit "A" revolves solidly between the the two large ball bearings on top or direct gear giving maximum efficiency.

(2). The lined selector and brake bands can be readily removed by taking off the top cover only.

(3). Adjustment to either band is instantaneously made by one or other of the two screwed plugs "B" respectively.

(4). In case of any necessary repair to the complete revolving unit it is only necessary to unbolt the central division of the gear box, when the complete revolving unit may be bodily lifted out leaving the gear box base chamber in the chassis, so avoiding any possibility of upsetting the gear box alignment.

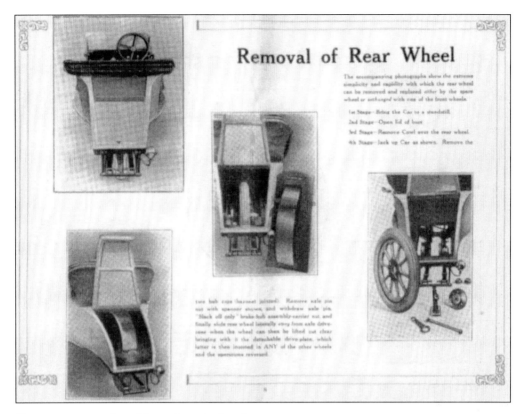

Illustrations reproduced from the sales brochure.

This Castle Three body shell was discovered in Brittany and brought back to England. It escaped the scrap man, but how it got there is a mystery.

There are probably only two Castle Threes that have survived, this one was discovered in Yorkshire. The car was purchased by the County Museum at Hartlebury early in 2002 and was collected from Yorkshire by Graham Turner (left) for the museum. The gentleman on the right is Dennis Garriock, the son of the previous owner, whose late husband Charlie Knight restored it.

Five

The Demolition
of Brinton's

The new millennium saw the town centre going through more changes with the demolition of the Brinton's factory. The factory had stood on this site for nearly 200 years and indeed a lot of the town had developed around it.

Brinton's in the mid-nineteenth century.

The Brinton's factory in 1998 from the Market Street multi-storey car park.

The Brinton's Carpet Company hold the proud position of being the oldest established carpet manufacturer in the oldest carpet-making town in the country, with a name that is known throughout the world. The factory has been situated in the centre of the town since the site was purchased in 1819, and a lot of the town has developed around the factory. It was therefore quite a shock to a lot of Kidderminster people when it was announced, towards the end of the twentieth century, that the factory at the Corporation Street site was going to be demolished.

In 1783 William Brinton founded his spinning industry at Hill Pool Village, then William's son, Henry, established the carpet factory near to the town centre to work in conjunction with the spinning firm. At that time the area of the factory was 4,118 square yards, by the 1930s it had grown to over 13 acres.

The firm's name has changed a number of times during its long history, the first change coming in 1848 when the name was changed to Henry Brinton & Sons when Henry's two sons, Henry and John, joined the firm. The two Henrys died in 1857 leaving the firm in the control of John.

In 1858 the name changed to Brinton & Lewis when a brother-in-law of John Brinton, named John Lewis, was taken into partnership. Around this time the spinning mill was transferred from Hill Pool to Kidderminster and the productive capacity increased. In 1870 the health of John Lewis deteriorated and so the partnership was dissolved, this resulted in another name change to John Brinton & Company, and then in 1881 to John Brinton & Company Ltd. In 1891, after the company had been enlarged and reconstructed, the name changed again to Brinton's Ltd. John Brinton passed away in 1914, aged eighty-seven, after sixty-six years with the company, in which time he had developed it enormously.

The factory in the 1930s, looking virtually as it did at the time of its demolition in 2001.

The site at Castle Road in 2000, with the factory emptied, awaiting demolition.

The site was chosen mainly for the river Stour, which ran right through and under the factory. After the factory had been demolished, Park Lane and Park Street could be viewed from Corporation Street.

The site from Castle Road Canal Bridge.

The bulldozers can be seen clearing the Corporation Street car park in readiness for the demolition of the Market Street multi-storey, 20 January 2001.

Demolition well under way, 6 February 2001. The multi-storey car park in Corporation Street is visible to the centre-right of the picture.

Corporation Street, 20 January 2001. The bus garage can be seen to the left shortly before it also was demolished.

Six

Town Centre Redevelopment

Looking from Coventry Street to the former site of the Kidderminster Brewery and Tower Buildings on right.

Pile driving was used to strengthen the banks of the river Stour prior to the building of Crown House. A large concrete slab was then placed across the river.

This was Trinity Lane Bridge with the old bridge in the background, December 1966.

In 1967 the Town Bridge was totally rebuilt, it was raised and the centre support column was removed to allow a clearer flow for the river.

After the rebuilding work was completed the site was made ready for the construction of Crown House. In the bottom right of the photograph can be seen the large slab which was placed over the river enabling the construction to sit on top; High Street can also be seen. At the time the shops between High Street and Swan Street had been demolished in preparation for the building of the Swan Centre. The car park in Blackwell Street (centre of the picture) had already been built. At the extreme right hand side can be seen the site for the Pitts Lane car park.

In the background can be seen the old premises of Foster's ironmongers. Their new premises, from after they had merged with Messrs Wise to become Foster & Wise Ltd, are on the left.

The site, ready for construction to begin. To alleviate the chance of further flooding, the Bull Ring area was raised by 5ft, hence the ramp down into Mill Street. When the greengrocers shop at 9 Lower Mill Street was constructed, planning was granted on the understanding that the first floor level would be set to allow for the possibility of Mill Street being raised in the future.

Crown House under construction, sitting on its concrete slab. It was opened on 1 August 1971, replacing the Exchange Street post office of 1885.

Crown House under construction, viewed from the proposed site of the Pitts Lane multi-storey.

A newly-constructed Crown House in 1971. Crown House has been the subject of much controversy in recent years, due mainly to its grubby appearance. When it was new it looked bright and clean but unfortunately the construction has not weathered very well.

The second multi-storey car park to be constructed in the town. It was built on the site of the former cotton mill in Pitts Lane and was opened 10 December 1971. Together with the multi-storey in Blackwell Street 2,260 parking spaces were provided.

The floors were constructed on site at ground level and then raised to the correct level by means of a screw jack fixed at each column. The process was known as 'lift slab' construction and was devised by the contractors Douglas. The car park was demolished in late 2001 at the same time as the third multi-storey in Market Street. There was a great outcry from the general public and shopkeepers alike due to the lack of parking facilities in the town.

This grand block of buildings fronting on Coventry Street was to become a casualty of the Swan Centre development. They were not so grand inside however; in the late 1950s I used to visit an elderly piano/violin teacher, Mildred Owen, who had turned her hand to giving guitar lessons to teenagers like myself who had been bitten by the Lonnie Donegan bug. A very dark and dingy staircase accessed her studio on the first floor, which was heated by a very antique-looking gas fire.

The mock-Tudor building seen here is Harvey's Bar or Vaults; it closed on 31 December 1967. It opened around 1855 and was originally known as The Clarence, then from 1887-1888 it was called The Fleece.

Here, the shops between High Street and Swan Street have just been demolished in preparation for the building of the Swan Centre. For a short time Swan Street was exposed to the daylight - it had always lived in the shadow of the High Street shops. On the right of the photograph you can see the old cellars, which have been uncovered by the demolition. The new Woolworths store was being built, top right, on the former site of the Lion Hotel.

The Kidderminster Brewery viewed from the upper level of Blackwell Street. To the left is the Black Star. The Black Star opened around 1820 and closed 17 September 1966. Blackwell Street was once known as Black Star Street.

Blackwell Street multi-storey was the first to be built in the town and was opened on 31 October 1969. It was built on the site of the Kidderminster Brewery, and in 2002 was once again the only multi-storey in the town.

The architects' model for the Swan Centre.

The Market Street multi-storey car park, 6 February 2001, just prior to its demolition. This was the last multi-storey car park to be built and when it was completed it was the boast of the planners that you could park in any of the three car parks and not have to walk more than 200 yards to any one of the major shops.

Seven

The Ring Road

Worcester Street in 1968, illustrating the unsuitability of the narrow streets for traffic passing through the town. In 1960 a traffic survey was conducted and it was recorded that on average 1,800 vehicles passed through the town centre each hour, and of this 64% was through-traffic. In 1962 the Borough Council decided to construct an inner ring road to take passing traffic away from the town centre; work began 2 August 1965.

Hall Street was between Church Street and The Horsefair. This was to be stage one of the ring road, and the street is seen here in 1966 just before the work began.

Stage one has been started, August 1966. Church Street is to the left, St Mary's church to the right, and Mill Street and The Black Horse Hotel can be seen at the top of the picture. A new bridge was put over the river Stour; the aqueduct on the right would have been constructed between the years of 1766 and 1772. The canal brought more prosperity to the town giving the carpet factories transport access to the river Severn, at newly-created Stourport, and then on to the ocean-going ships at Bristol.

Stage one of the ring road, bisecting Church Street, September 1966.

The remains of the top section of Church Street, 1966. Dr J.R. Craig lived in one of these houses, he was part-time medical officer for Kidderminster from 1922 until 1946. During the Second World War he was in charge of casualty services.

Putting the top surface on stage one. The Royal George can be seen in the background; opening around 1793 it remained after the initial construction of the ring road, but closed on 10 October 1973, having survived for 180 years.

The Royal George in splendid isolation after the opening of stage one.

This was Blackwell Street at the junction of Waterloo Street and is now where the island between Blackwell Street and the Horsefair is situated (see below).

Stage one almost complete, 1967.

The demolition of 17-18 Church Street, 1968.

Stage one was completed and opened to traffic in May 1967, at a cost of £477,000. This included the bridge over the river Stour and a section of under-road heating. A new paved area was constructed in front of St Mary's church replacing the top end of Church Street. The under-road heating was eventually abandoned as it proved too troublesome.

Stage one can be seen running from the left of the picture to the circle, which is the island in Coventry Street. Stage two runs from this island to the island on Comberton Hill. At the bottom left is Blackwell Street and Tower Buildings.

Stage two was constructed between January 1969 and March 1971 at a cost of £955,000. To the left of the island is the bottom end of Worcester Street with the Law Court, and at the extreme bottom left of the picture can be seen the Central cinema in Oxford Street.

Aerial view from the 1930s. From left to right: Bromsgrove Street, Anchorfields, and George Street.

The Worcester Cross Hotel on the corner of Hoo Road and Comberton Hill in 1968. The Playhouse can be seen to the middle left of the picture. The Worcester Cross opened around 1828 and was closed on the 4 January 1969 in preparation for the second and third stages of the ring road. On the left hand side of the picture at No. 4, Comberton Road, almost opposite to the Worcester Cross was the Clarendon public house, opened around 1855 but closed on the 20 October 1959 before this photograph was taken. Just along Hoo Road on the left was another public house, The Leopard; this was another casualty of the ring road, opening around 1820 and closing May 1968.

Stage two nearly complete. Bromsgrove Street joined Comberton Hill roughly at this point; it now ends at the Glades arena.

The rear of the Victoria Carpet Factory in 1972, just prior to the work commencing on stage three of the ring road.

The rear of the council depot in Green Street, 1972.

Looking toward Worcester Road from the direction of the Comberton Hill island (below Aggborough), 1972.

July 1972 and stage three is underway. The side of Hoo Hill below Aggborough had to be dug away, and the river Stour had to be crossed by a 6.27m span. To the right is a part of the factories which were demolished in the Green Street development of 2001-02.

The river Stour was diverted through this culvert and then covered in earth.

After the hill had been dug away a retaining wall 320m long and up to 11m high had to be built.

Stage three making good progress, 1972. There are at least ten stacks in this shot of the factories facing Green Street; by 2002 they had all disappeared.

Looking toward Worcester Road island, in the background is Bradley & Turton's factory and beyond Brinton Park.

There have been no problems with the retaining wall in the thirty years since it was constructed.

The opening of the third stage, 17 August 1973 by Keith Speed MP, linking Comberton Hill (A448) to the Worcester Road (A456), built at a cost of £1,700,000. A car park was installed on the site of the Worcester Road island. With spaces for 300 cars, it provided ideal parking for the factory workers in Green Street. At certain times of the year a funfair would be installed on the island, in earlier times it had been accommodated in the old cattle market in Market Street and sometimes on Brinton's Park. At the time of writing the council had made no decision where future funfairs would be held.

The Comberton Hill end of stage three looking clean and new.

Stage four showing Bewdley Street to Mill Street. The Gilt Edge factory (centre-left) was formerly Carpet Trades and was at one time the town's largest employer. The factory was demolished in 1993 when it had been taken over by Coloroll.

This was Crowther Street (Bethesda Street before 1877) which disappeared when stage four of the ring road was constructed. The parade was for the opening of the new St John's church hall by the Revd W.A. Trippass, 24 April 1954. It consisted of the 4th Kidderminster Company of the Boys Brigade (run for many years by Mr and Mrs Crick of Birchfield Road) and St John's church choir led by Mr E. Forshaw. The previous church hall, which had been built in 1897, had been badly damaged by fire. The cross bearer is Mr Knowles. The choirboys, from right to left: E. Chatwin, B. Arnold, D. Mansfield (partly hidden), D. Smith, R. Barber, A. Knott, D, Lucas, -?-, B. Thomas, ? Robinson, -?-, -?-. The men's choir includes Mr Pagett, Pete Hazelwood, Mr Knowles Jnr, and Mr Oliver.

Proud Cross looking towards Mason Road. This is the site of the island at the end of stage four leading to Franche.

Eight

Firemen

The main appliance room of Kidderminster Fire Station, *c.* 1930.

The first large authority to establish a proper fire brigade in the United Kingdom was Edinburgh in 1824. Five years later the first steam fire engine was introduced, built by John Braithwaite of London. It was quite limited in design features, having only a very limited success, and by 1833 production had ceased. Any appliance of any size at this time would have been horse drawn, as was the case for many more years to come. Engineering techniques were improving all the time, however, and in 1858 Shand Mason & Company produced another steam engine due in some part to a revitalised interest from the people running the fire brigades.

The fire-fighting arrangements in the mid-nineteenth century were a very complicated affair with no one single authority being in charge of procedures. There were brigades manned by the police forces, there were insurance brigades and some volunteer brigades. Some large country estates made their own arrangements due to the length of time it took other brigades to arrive at their properties.

The Kidderminster Fire Brigade, 1896. The fire station at this time was situated at the rear of the town hall. The situation in Kidderminster was no different to anywhere else at the time in that before 1876 the Fire Assurance Offices provided the fire-fighting appliances for the town. Some companies would provide the policyholder with a badge, which was attached to the insured building to show that particular building was insured with their company, so if a company's badge was not displayed, the relevant fire fighters would not turn out. The badge for the Norwich Union (top left) is displayed on a building in the High Street in Bewdley; I have never seen one in Kidderminster. The Birmingham Fire Office supplied the town with a fire-fighting appliance in 1841; this was kept in Oxford Street by the market entrance gates. Another followed in 1845 from the Royal Farmers Assurance, and one in 1868 from the Norwich Union; this one was stored in the old savings bank at the corner of Callows Lane. A number of the carpet factories would have had their own fire-fighting arrangements due to the high risk of fire that was present in their premises.

A volunteer fire brigade was formed in 1876 consisting of twelve members who were led by the borough engineer. The fire engine was kept in a house at the top of Church Street but then was moved to the rear of the Town Hall in 1877. The reason Brinton's Bull – a steam whistle that was used to call people to work – was installed in 1882 was to act as an alarm in the event of a fire. The council gave permission for its use from 3 May 1882, and the following code was arranged: one blast for a borough fire, two for a fire in the foreign, and three for a fire at Brinton's works. This was the perk for Brinton's having installed the warning system, ensuring that in the event of a fire at their factory they were guaranteed prompt attention with their own personal signal, a smart move. This was the norm for many years and when improved communication methods rendered its continued use unnecessary it was retained as a timekeeper. It was last sounded in 1999.

Captain W.M. Hughes, chief officer of the Kidderminster brigade in the early twentieth century. Captain Hughes was an electrical engineer and specialized in supplying and fitting industrial electrical motors, a lot of the carpet factories were converting to electricity at this time to drive their machinery. He fitted Astley Hall, the home of Prime Minister Stanley Baldwin, with electric lighting, and soon afterwards Baldwin made the rather witty observation in one of his speeches: 'Old Hughes fitted my home with electric lighting then promptly joined the fire brigade.'

When the Kidderminster brigade had the horse-drawn appliance, one of the firemen, Mr Dalloe, lived at the top of Castle Road. When the alarm sounded he would send his son Jim off down to a paddock in the area where the Worcester Road island was to be in later years, to fetch the horses. He in turn would rush off to the town hall to get the engine ready; this was fitted with a pair of specially-designed horses' collars (visible behind the engine in the picture on the previous page) which were already attached to the appliance. They were simply slipped over the horses heads and were then ready for the off, saving valuable minutes. Mr Dalloe's son later joined the brigade and can be seen on the picture of the opening of the new station in Castle Road.

An extract from the *Kidderminster Shuttle*, 15 December 1906:

'Excellent response by Fire Brigade. Exactly at half past three o'clock on Monday morning P.C. Bouckley, who was on duty in the Bull Ring, noticed smoke issuing from the upper premises of the Melias Stores, and a moment afterwards a blaze was seen. Bouckley instantly gave an alarm, the fire bells were rung, and within five minutes some members of the Fire Brigade were at the police station, [the police station at that time was situated in Vicar Street close to the town hall] and rushed off with the reel hose. It is satisfactory to record that within seven minutes of the fire being discovered members of the Fire Brigade were pouring a stream of water on the building. The firemen, who worked exceedingly well under the direction of Captain Hughes and Lieutenant Phipps, made commendable efforts to save the adjoining buildings, and in this they were successful. At one time it seemed as though the whole block of buildings would be enveloped but the streams of water were so well directed that the flames were unable to spread to either side. The building belongs to the Grammar School.'

Melia's store in the Bull Ring.

The foundations for St George's church were begun on 19 July 1821, the day that King George IV was crowned king. It cost a little over £18,000, of which £2,000 was raised locally. The church was consecrated on 13 September 1824. It was one of the 'Waterloo' or 'Commissioners' churches. This was the name given to churches that were the subject of a grant from the government. Soon after the end of the Napoleonic Wars, Parliament voted to grant £1,000,000 for the building of churches in populated areas, and St George's was one of these. The interior was galleried and rather ornate. In the early days of St George's church the firm of Bowyers wove a beautiful altar-piece depicting the 'Descent from the Cross'. Sadly this was vandalised in 1826 and never replaced. On the evening of Sunday 9 November 1886 a census of worshippers was carried out at the Kidderminster churches, with the results being published in the *Kidderminster Shuttle* on 13 November 1886. There were a total of 5,883 worshippers in Kidderminster that Sunday, which represented 21% of Kidderminster's population. St George's totalled 1,093, while St Mary's was second with 751. The complete list can be found in *Kidderminster*, Tomkinson and Hall, or on microfilm in Kidderminster Reference Library.

On 20 November 1922 the church was badly damaged by fire, with the interior being completely destroyed and only the walls and tower left standing. My late mother was eleven years old at the time and lived at the Horsefair Tavern in Stourbridge Road. She often told me how the bell crashed down inside the tower and woke half the neighbourhood. The church was rebuilt within three years but took on a more lofty appearance, as the ornate galleries were not replaced. Selling postcards of the church similar to the picture above raised some funds that went toward the cost of repairs.

From left to right, back row: W. Toon. -?-, T. Pearsall, J. Dalloe Jnr, -?-. Middle row: Officer Blencowe, Harry Owen, Harold Routley, Herbert Cooper. Front row: 2nd Officer, Lt French, Capt Hughes, Frank Cope, Mayor George Eddy, -?-, C. Pearsall, Ted Bath.

The Pearsall family appear to have always had some member of their family in the Kidderminster Brigade, starting with Charles Pearsall Snr. Various family members after Charles have been: Tom Pearsall (brother), Ted Farr (brother-in-law), Charles Pearsall Jnr (son), John Pearsall (grandson) and David Pearsall (great-grandson). David was a member of the brigade at the time of writing in 2002.

As there is some uncertainty with some of the names above here is a list of the Kidderminster Brigade as at April 1930;

Name & Rank	Age	Years service
W.M. Hughes, Chief Officer	53	24
E. French 2nd Officer	66	30
F.W. Cope Fireman	49	24
T. Barth, driver and electrician	48	16
W. Blencowe, engineer	44	18
F. Tolley, fireman	65	14
Dalloe Snr, driver horse and motor	54	20
H. Routley, fireman	36	9
C. Pearsall Sn, fireman	52	15
C. Pearsall Jnr, fireman	27	2
Cope Jnr, fireman	27	2
Dalloe Jnr, fireman	26	9
Turnock T. Carter	70	35+
H. Owen, station engineer	36	9

It was reported in the *Kidderminster Shuttle* on 5 January 1929 that the town council had decided upon the erection of a new fire station in Castle Road. The building was to consist of a compact two-storey block at a total cost of £4,000. On the ground floor there was to be a large engine station 40ft by 30ft in three bays, with equipment stores and a bathroom for the use of the firemen. On the first floor, accommodation for the resident station engineer was planned, along with a large recreation room and an office for the station captain.

The hose-drying tower, fitted with hose rollers, was to be 42ft high with ample washing space at the rear of the station. A garden was also included for the station engineer. The whole of the new building would be centrally heated on the low pressure hot water system.

The tender of Messrs Bridgwater Bros, Cradley Heath Staffs, for the building work at £3,657 had been accepted. The Mayor E.G. Eddy, JP, and deputy Mayor J.E. Grosvenor T.D, laid ceremonial foundation stones on 15 April 1929.

The main appliance room in 1929.

Reference to Brinton's Bull: a letter from Chief Officer to Watch Committee, 5 August 1930.

"At 2 a.m. this morning I was informed on the phone by Police Inspector Bint, Kidderminster, of a fire at Broadheath Worcester.

Owing to my brigade being depleted by a few men on holiday and one sick, also absence of steam for blowing 'bull'* during the week to obtain Works Brigades assistance, I decided not to turn out.'

About 15 minutes later a message from Inspector Timms, Worcester County Police H.Q., stated that a garage was on fire and cars were destroyed, and there was no further danger. Also Worcester City Brigade would not attend as it was outside their area."

*The Editor understands that the phrase containing this word means a steam operated warning device to call in private/retained fire crews, and would like more information.

The opening ceremony. On the left is the Mayor E.G. Eddy, and on the right the deputy Mayor J.E. Grosvenor with their respective wives.

The funeral cortege wending its way along Wood Street is probably that of Captain Hughes. The 2nd fireman from the front left is C. Pearsall.

The Auxiliary Fire Service on a wet church parade. Third from front right is W. Smith and fifth is J. Foxall. There were rapid developments between the two world wars and by the late 1930s there were hundreds of brigades but very few professional fire fighters, in fact just over 4,000 in the UK The remainder were volunteer and retained fire fighters. In April 1938 the AFS had over 20,000 pumps available and 30,000 firemen had been recruited, boosting the number of full-time fire fighters to almost 10,000 overnight.

From twenty fire reports taken at random from the Station Log Book for 1937:
9 were domestic chimney or soot related 45%
3 faulty electrical wiring 15%
3 motor vehicles 15%
The other 5 were all different incidents.

The commonest cause of domestic fires today is from cooking, especially involving chip and grill pans.

A makeshift water tender for the Second World War consisting of a flatbed lorry with an inflatable water reservoir mounted on the back. In the early days of the Second World War friction was evident between the auxiliaries and the regular firemen, but the main problem was still the equipment incompatibility. This was overcome in the short term by the manufacture of adapters for different sizes of hose couplings etc. The AFS soon proved their worth as the blitz intensified and people's attitudes towards them were completely turned round.

On 22 May 1941 the National Fire Service (NFS) was formed in an attempt to unify the whole of the country's fire brigades. At the same time the Treasury ordered 2,000 Austin K2 towing vehicles (ATVs). After the war the Fire Services Act 1947 was placed on the statute book. This resulted in the dissolution of the National Fire Service with brigades reverting back to the control of the local authorities. Changes to local government arrangements in 1974 saw borough brigades being incorporated into central county brigades and some brigades were renamed after further changes in 1985.

An inspection by the mayor with the brigade wearing their Second World War issue helmets.

Some members of the NFS.

Fears of nuclear war in the 1950s saw the Green Goddesses of the AFS brought back into service. The fears eventually receded and they were put back into storage in 1968, but they have been used on a few occasions since, one time being the firemen's strike during the 1970s.

Kidderminster is a part of the Hereford & Worcester Fire Brigade.

Fire drill in the 1950s at the rear of the Kidderminster station. The appliance is a Fordson heavy pumping unit with wheeled escape and was designed by the Home Office for the Second World War.

Red Watch, 1979, photographed to commemorate the fiftieth anniversary of the fire station in Castle Road. The appliance is a Carmichael S. & D., of which only three were made. From left to right: J. Pearsall (sub officer), T. Pyle (leading fireman), P. Collins (fireman), M. Turbutt (fireman), F. Fawkes (fireman), A. Vernalls (fireman), A. Humphries (fireman), J. Head (leading fireman).

Presentation of a certificate by the RSPCA for rescuing a horse from the river Stour at Clensmore, October 1983. From left to right: firemen Twinner, Donaldson, Cope and Milroy, leading fireman Cook, fireman Jagoda, G. Harrison of the RSPCA, -?-, firemen Forsbrook, Murphy, Williams and Richards, leading fireman Brown, Station Officer McGough.

The Hereford & Worcester Fire Brigade employs four main types of staff: full time fire-fighters, retained fire fighters, fire control operators and support staff. The basic training for fire fighters is sixteen weeks, with a probationary period of two years.

Waiting for the next alarm call. The latest style of helmet was introduced in 2001.

The brigade sometimes makes presentations; here W.J. Logan Jnr is presented with a certificate from the Society for the Protection of Life From Fire, by the Hereford & Worcester Fire Brigade for rescuing three colleagues from an upper floor during a fire at the Sugar Factory, Foley Park, with total disregard for his own safety. Chief Fire Officer G. Eastham is in the centre.

Trophy presented to The Hereford & Worcester Fire Brigade in 1989. Firemen don't just fight fires, they can be involved in anything from traffic accidents and animal rescues, to pulling people out of sewers. The latter resulted in the above trophy being presented by the BBC Television programme '999'.

HOME OFFICE

CHIP PANS CAN HURT, MAIM, OR KILL. PLEASE TAKE CARE.

The majority of domestic fires are caused by cooking accidents, especially from chip pans.

They like to keep their fire engine clean, March 2002. The Dennis Sabre, including all its apparatus, costs in the region of £200,000.

Kidderminster Fire Station, 17 March 2002. The vehicles in the centre and left are the Dennis Sabre Water/Ladder built by Carmichael, and on the right is a Leyland Daf Water Carrier with a capacity of 9,000 litres.

Nine

Caldwall Tower

From a postcard dated 13 September 1907. Excavations were carried out at Caldwall in 1961 soon after the house in the above picture was demolished due to having fallen into disrepair. Kidderminster and District Archaeological and Historical Society seized the once in a lifetime opportunity and found many items in the dig, which continued for three seasons. The oldest artefact unearthed was a Saxon shield boss; there was pottery of all periods from Norman to modern day, and a penny of Edward II from which the date of the hall is based. In its heyday Caldwall was probably similar to Stokesay Castle, between Ludlow and Craven Arms in Shropshire.

It became clear that the demolished house was the last of a series of buildings that had stood on the site, being built around the tower in about 1700. The tower, which had been built in the fourteenth century, was connected by a short corridor to a hall of two storeys built in the same period. This in turn had been built across the eastern end of an earlier arcaded hall. Around 1700 everything except the tower seems to have been demolished; the houses were then subsequently built.

The Hall had many uses during the twentieth century. It had belonged to the borough since the late nineteenth century when they had purchased it from George Turton in 1897 - the main reason being to put a much-needed road bridge across the river Stour and canal. The building has also been used as a domestic science centre, offices for the medical officer of the Health and Education Department and during the Second World War it was used by the ARP.

The area that was excavated is probably only one-eighth of the area that lies hidden beneath the castle road and surrounding buildings. The tower appears to have had a charmed life; it was restored and reopened in 1970 and it was stated in the literature presented at the opening that the tower was now preserved for future generations. Unfortunately the tower was neglected and fell into a very sorry state and for some time there was speculation of what was to become of the monument.

Caldwall Mill, first mentioned in the fourteenth century, must have been enlarged in the industrial revolution. In 1847 Cuthbert Bede wrote of, 'Caldwall looking pretty beside its lengthened lake', which in 1859 stretched to the doors of Caldwall Hall.

It would appear the basement room of the tower (or to give it its corrected name of the 'under croft') had its floor level raised before 1700, probably because of the lengthening of the lake for Caldwall Mill.

Mr Richard Davies, in the guise of a knight in shining armour, came to the rescue of the Caldwall Tower when he purchased it early in 1998. It was in a neglected state with the under croft being full of decaying carpet and rotting furniture; there were also a lot of metal chairs left over from the Second World War and large lumps of concrete. He set to straight away in the dirty and unpleasant task of removing all this unwanted rubble, and over a period of some three and half years has faithfully restored the tower to probably better than its former glory, and in so doing has made sure that it will survive for many years to come.

Caldwall Mill, c. 1931.

Caldwall Tower, 10 February 2002.

The under croft.

The under croft, now in pristine condition and probably cleaner than it has ever been in its 700-year existence.

The first floor. Mr Davies has gone to great lengths in researching the heraldry of the people who have been connected with Caldwall over the centuries and has had portraits of previous owners faithfully copied.

It is quite amazing how habitable the tower has been made; walking or driving past one could not possibly imagine how delightful the interior now is.

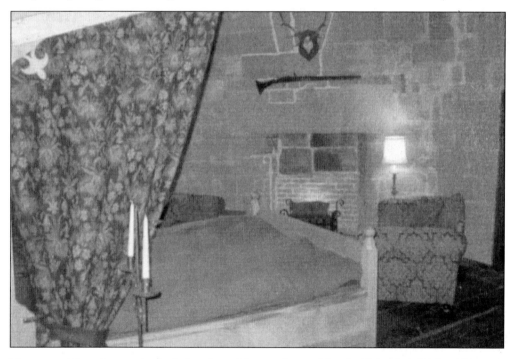

The second floor is now the bed chamber with en-suite washing facilities. It is Richard Davies's intention to open the tower to the public from time to time and it is well worth a visit as he will be able to relate to you in great detail its history. These few photographs only give a vague impression of what the tower is really like.

The Kidderminster Rifle Club, formed 1902, on the occasion of winning the Astor Challenge Cup for Worcestershire on 29 June 1904. Lord Astor presented the Astor Cups to all the counties in England in 1902, to be competed for by the respective rifle clubs. It is still competed for today. From left to right, back row: W.M. Hughes, T.W. Baylis, Dr W. Hodgson Moore, F.W. Davies, A.J. Foster (Foster's ironmongers). Front row: R.E. Grove, H. Hill, E. Pugh; J.H. Smith (J. Herbert Smith, builders).

Acknowledgements

I am indebted to the following for the use of photographs, information, interest, time, and patience:

Jeff Higgott (Council Services, Town Centre Development, The Ring Road); Shaun Licence; Mike Cale; Gavin and Stuart Logan; Mrs P. Vaughan (The Sugar Factory); Ms Vaudin (Clement Dalley); Mrs Barbara Naylor; Mrs D. Clee; Mrs Judy Vale (T. & A Naylor); The Hereford & Worcester Fire Brigade, Station Officer Dave Williams, John and David Pearsall (firemen); Mr Richard Davies (Caldwall Tower); Bob Young; Goff Jones (Castle Motor Co.); G. Edwards (Smethwick Drop Forgings); David Duffield (various postcards); Terry Jackson (Kidderminster Rifle Club); Mrs J. Jackson (introduction to Mrs Naylor).